NEW IDENTITY

By

Daramola Joel Odunayo

Tel: 08033275896, 07028206482

ISBN: 9798374619713

Published by

CHRIST THE REDEEMER'S MINISTRIES

1-9, Redemption Way, P.M.B. 1088, Ebute Metta, Lagos, Nigeria.

Unless otherwise stated, all scriptural quotation are from the Authorized King James Version of the Holy Bible.

Printed in Nigeria by: **CRM PRESS**

KM 46 Lagos-Ibadan Expressway, CRM Shopping Complex, Back of Old Auditorium, Redemption Camp,

Tel: 08077833792, 08069452037

E-mail: crmpress@yahoo.com

TABLE OF CONTENTS

DEDICATION

This book is dedicated to our Lord Jesus Christ; my Savior and the Holy Spirit my senior partner in life and ministry and my heavenly Father, the Almighty God (YAHWEH) and to my father in the Lord, Pastor E. A. Adeboye

and to everyone that is tired of watching enemies enjoy what belong to them and ready to fight to recover them all, also to everyone that attends 'Power Service' our weekly breakthrough and deliverance service in various locations.

ACKNOWLEDGEMENT

I appreciate the efforts of everybody who at different stages contributed immensely to the success of this book. Also my sincere regards and appreciation go to my better half that helped me in typing the book, and Pastor Aremu of CRM Press who took time to read through the manuscript to make very useful adjustment and many others that helped in making this dream to become a reality.

INTRODUCTION

In Christ Jesus, we are given a new identity. We are no longer defined by our past mistakes or by the labels that society has placed upon us. Instead, we are given the righteousness of Christ and are made into a new creation (2 Corinthians 5:17).

Ephesians 2:10 states, "For we are his workmanship, created in Christ Jesus for good works, which God prepared beforehand, that we should walk in them." We are God's handiwork, created anew in Jesus for a purpose.

In Christ, we are given a new identity as children of God (John 1:12). We are no longer slaves to sin, but have been set free to live in righteousness (Romans 6:18). We are no longer defined by our past, but by our new identity in Jesus.

When we accept Jesus as our Lord and Savior, we are given a new identity. We are no longer defined by our past mistakes, our failures, or our limitations. We are no longer bound by the labels that society has placed upon us or by the expectations of others. We are now children of God, free to live our lives according to His plan and purpose.

Our new identity in Christ Jesus is one of righteousness, holiness, and grace. We are forgiven of our sins and made pure in the eyes of God. We have access to the power of the Holy Spirit, who guides us and empowers us to live a life that is pleasing to God. We are no longer slaves to our own sinful nature, but have been set free to live in righteousness.

With our new identity, we are given a new purpose and a new mission. We are called to love God and love others, to share the good news of salvation with those around us, and to make a positive impact on the world. We are equipped with the gifts and talents that God has given us to serve Him and His kingdom.

Our new identity in Christ Jesus is something to be celebrated, embraced, and lived out to the fullest. It is a gift from God that brings joy, peace, and fulfillment. It is something that we can take pride in, and it gives us hope for the future. We are no longer who we were, but we are who God has created us to be, a new creation in Christ Jesus.

CHAPTER 1: MY TIME OF NEW WINE

As Christians, we are expected to drink the new wine but most Christians feed on leftovers that are not the desire of God for them. Looking at the story of the marriage at Cana of Galilee, it was evident that the couples were helpless but when the One who can meet all our needs steps in, the wine that finished was more than enough. Infact, the miraculous wine they got was the best. Let us look at the account of the wedding in Cana of Galilee which Jesus attended with his mother.

And the third day there was a marriage in Cana of Galilee; and the mother of Jesus was there: And both Jesus was called, and his disciples, to the marriage. And when they wanted wine, the mother of Jesus saith unto him, they have no wine .but Jesus saith unto her, Woman, what have I to do with thee? Mine hour is not yet come. His mother saith unto the servants, whatsoever he saith unto you, do it .And there were set there six water pots of stone, after the manner of the purifying of the Jews, containing two or three firkins apiece. Jesus saith unto them fill the water pots with water. And they filled them up to the brim. .And he saith unto them, Draw out now, and bear unto the governor of the feast and they bare it. When the ruler of the feast had tasted the water that was made wine, and knew not whence it was: (but the servants that drew the water knew) the governor of the feast called the bridegroom. And saith unto him, every man at the beginning doth set forth good wine; and when men have well drunk, then that which is worse: but thou has kept the good wine until now. This beginning of miracles did Jesus in Cana of Galilee, and manifested forth his glory; and his disciples believed on him.

The account above is the story of a man and woman who was about to start enjoying their life in marriage but suddenly their wine finished, their source of income (employment terminated) dried up, their joy was mixed with sorrow on their wedding day. God intervened and they had a new beginning. Has your source suddenly dried or has your helper dumped you or perhaps your companion deserted you?

IT IS YOUR TURN FOR A NEW WINE

Until the old wine finishes, the new wine will not come. Old wine is whatever you achieve with your own strength, effort and ability inotherwords, personal achievement, educational degree or when you are buoyant financially. Nobody appreciates something new, unless the old is turns sour. Every good movie has a part 1 and 2. The first part is always full of trouble and pain but the second part is full of excitement and recovery. This season is part two of your life.

Attributes of old wine.

It make happy and also proud. Judges 9:12-13.

It brings worldly celebration that leads to captivity. Isaiah 39:1-8, Luke 12:16-21.

It intoxicates and opens doors to immorality. Genesis 19:32-38.

It leads to misbehaviour and brings curses to someone's house. Genesis 9:20-27.

It opens door to enemy attacks. 2 Samuel 13:28.

It can finish at a critical stage. 1 Samuel 2:9.

Attributes of new wine

New wine is a product of Divine intervention.

New wine is a product of Divine sovereignty. Psalm 115:3 & 33:8-9.

New wine is a product of Divine creativity.

New wine is a product of Divine response to human needs.

HOW TO GET IT

First, you can get new wine when you completely obey without complaints. Luke 9:61-62. Second, you have to cooperate with God and

His mission. Third, you have to be fast in your response to God's demands (if you want your Lazarus to rise, then roll away the stone). Finally, before your wine finishes invite Jesus first to your life.

NEW WINE WILL GIVE YOU

New wine will give you Divine health as contained in Exodus 15:26 & 23, 24-27. It is always available as Deuteronomy 28:1-3 exemplified, it has no side effects and it lasts forever.

YOUR NEW WINE IS NOW

As a child of God, you have to stand out and you've got to things the way God wants it. Many bible characters were divinely favoured and have remained a reference point for years. Virgin Mary was divinely favoured and she became the mother of the saviour of the world. The Almighty God Divinely connected David and he became king over the Israelites and our Lord Jesus Christ came from his lineage. In the case of Joseph, it was Divine commission. Queen Esther received the mercy of God and she became a queen. The thief on the cross received divine mercy and made heaven. Obededom was divinely repositioned when the ark of God was in his house. Prophet Elisha was divinely transformed after he saw his master being taken by a whirlwind. Saul had a divine turnaround when he met Christ on his way to Damascus and became an Apostle.

YOU CANNOT PUT A NEW WINE INSIDE AN OLD BOTTLE

It is an abomination to put new wine into an old bottle. The bible attest to this in Matthew9:16 - 17. *"No man putteth a piece of new cloth unto an old garment, for that which is put in to fill it up taketh from the garment, and the rent is made worse. Neither do men put new wine into old bottles: else the bottles break, and the wine runneth out, and the bottles perish: but they put new wine into new bottles, and both are preserved".*

Also in Mark 2:21-23, the bible also uses the analogy of why mixing the old and new together will not work and give the desired result. Let us consider this. *"No man also seweth a piece of new cloth on an old garment: else the new piece that filled it up taketh away from the old, and the rent is made worse. And no man putteth new wine into old bottles: else the new wine doth burst the bottles, and the wine is spilled, and the bottles will be marred: but new wine must be put into new bottles. And it came to pass, that he went through the corn fields on the Sabbath day; and his disciples began, as they went, to pluck the ears of corn"*

What the above bible passages is telling us is that when we are born again; we do away with the old nature and take up the new nature of Christ. We are not expected to do things the way we do it before but to be Christ-like in nature.

CHAPTER 2: DRESS THE WAY YOU WANT TO BE ADDRESSED

In the book of Genesis, Adam and Eve, the first human being, realized they were naked after they ate an apple from the tree of knowledge. They were ashamed of their nakedness, and they made clothes for themselves out of fig leaves. As late as the 19th century, most Europeans and Americans believed that people wore clothing primarily for reasons of modesty.

The earliest clothing was made from animal skins and fur- as far back as 30,000 years ago. While fur and leather are still used to make some things, most articles of clothing are now made out of other fabrics.

You have the DNA of Christ in you and you are His masterpiece. Dress in a way that will depict you as a Christian and a worthy representative of Christ because you are addressed the way you dress.

It is heart breaking to see that the church is getting worldly in their dressing. 1st Peter 3:3-4 admonishes us to dress moderately. Dress well, attractively, decently to enhance and complement your body structure. Above all, dress to please and glorify your Lord and Master Jesus Christ.

DRESSING AND OUR APPEARANCE CAUSES LOTS OF DISPUTES IN A MARRIAGE

Some dress like slaves, immature, shabby, dress to kill, to attract, to seduce, arrogantly, like harlots, like masquerade and some are too extravagant. How do you dress, why did you dress that way and if Christ returns will you go with Him like this?

God is the first fashion designer but what is God's intention? Is your dress portraying your salvation? When you dress, put on righteousness of God.

I was just wondering why people wear clothes, what made people wear clothes in the first place? Why isn't your head declared as a private part or your hands declared as a private part?

PURPOSE OF DRESS

First, we wear clothe for warmth. Secondly, we wear clothes to cover our shame and nakedness. Thirdly, to make us look good and to protect our body from the effect of the environment (To protect us from bad weather).

IF EVERYONE IN YOUR ENVIRONMENT IS BLIND, WOULD YOU STILL DRESS THAT WAY?

A society's economic structure and its culture, or traditions and way of life, also influence the clothing that its people wear. In many societies, religious laws regulated personal behaviour.

Pride and extravagance in dressing is a sin to which women are especially prone. Hence the injunction of the Apostle relates directly to her: "In like manner also, that woman adorns themselves in modest apparel, with shamefacedness and sobriety; not with braided hair, or gold, or pearls, or costly array; but (which becometh women professing to be followers of God) with good works." 1Timothy 2:9-10

IF IT WAS FOR WARMTH

The hands and face can be exposed because covering them limits their use. It is purely because clothes protect you from the cold and from the sun (protection from the sun particularly important for white people). Unlike other mammals, we don't have the luxury of having skin that protects us from very hot or very cold weather temperatures. Our skin burns very easily under very hot temperatures and we can freeze to death if we are exposed to very low temperatures. Human beings have worn garments around their bodies since the ice age, because if we didn't; we would become extinct and died from frost bite. Your head / hands are not considered private parts because they do not expose our sexual body-parts in which are covered by ones underwear.

In Genesis 3:28-36, the Bible gives us a good gist concerning the mind of God about us- his creatures. He created us to exercise dominion over all things. I believe this includes our self-will, taste and discretion. Moreover, after the Creator had settled everything about creation. He adjudged that the exercise was very good. Gen.3:31 "*And God saw everything that He had made and behold, it was good*"'. It is quite disturbing today to see even Christians, male or female, married and unmarried dress in a way that is out of tune with God's intention. Men and women who profess to be born again are going out of their ways to embrace nudity. Looking at the way some of our Christian Sisters dress today to some of our places of worship is becoming embarrassing and shameful. Some have even decided to carry this terrible act to the altar of God. Like bush fire during the harmattan season, nudity is gradually taking over our land.

Unfortunately, some "modern day Christians" are not seeing it in this perspective. This set of people seems not to be aware that the body they are carrying about is the temple of God. 1

Cor.3:16-17 says "*know ye not that ye are the temple of God and that the Holy spirit of God dwell in you. "If any man defile the temple of God, him shall God destroy".* If you defile yourself, and pollute the sacred temple of God with what you wear all you are looking for is divine destruction.

Besides the promotion of nudity, another area of concern is the flagrant disobedience to the word of God in Duet 22:3 "women must not wear men's clothes, nor a man wears women's clothes, for the Lord detests anyone who does this".

The Bible does not contain the word of God. It is wrong to say the bible contains the word of God. Rather, the bible is the word of God. The container is different from the substance. A bucket is a container holding water or liquid. When you finish using the water, you keep the bucket. The two are different items. This is not so with the bible. The Bible is not a container but the real word. If this is the case, whatever the Bible says about your life and mine is final.

Anyone, anywhere can say anything, it does not matter. The word of God is the ultimate. God says it is an abomination for a man to wear what belongs to a woman or a woman to wear that, which is designed for men.

Are we saying God is not aware of our cultural backgrounds? *Love not the world, neither the things that are therein.* Any type of dress or designs that can make the opposite sex begin to think beyond the ordinary about your figure is ungodly. Ezekiel 16:13-16 says "*Thou was thou decked with gold and silver, and thy raiment was of fine linen and silk and embroiled milk...And thy renown went forth among the heathen for thy beauty, for it was perfect though my comeliness, which I had put on thee, and the Lord God. But thou trust in thine own beauty and playedst the harlot there upon...*" It is the glory of God upon your life that makes you beautiful or handsome. Your new outlook should not be of ordinary silver or gold but that given by the one who created you in his own image.

How you are dressed determines how you are received or treated. Your dressing is a part of your identity. How you dress equally affects your Kingdom walk. In 2 Kings 1:1-8, when the king was sick, he sent some people to enquire if he would recover or die. They met Elijah who told them that it was a sickness unto death. In order to verify the authenticity of that prophecy, the king asked for the name of the prophet but they could not tell because he did not disclose his name but by the time they described the type of clothes he wore, the king immediately knew it was Elijah.

Does your dressing portray you as a child of God? If you as a minister of God were to dress in regular clothes and not priestly robe or cassock- would your dressing showcase you as a servant of the Most High God?

If you compare what John the Baptist wore in Matthew 3:1-4 with what Elijah wore, you would find some resemblance. Who do you resemble when you dress? How is your hair done? What of your beard? How do you adorn yourself with jewellery – moderate or loud? What kind of dresses do you put on?

When Moses fled from Egypt to Midian after killing one of the Egyptians, he met the daughters of the priest of Midian and helped them. When they got home earlier than usual, their father asked why they were back home so soon. They said it was because they received protection and help from an Egyptian (Exodus 2:15-20).

Exodus 2:19 And they said, An Egyptian delivered us out of the hand of the shepherds, and also drew water enough for us, and watered the flock.

He was taken for an Egyptian because he dressed like one. If you dress like the world, what follows worldly attires will equally follow you. Worldly fashion is controlled by the lust of the flesh, the lust of the eyes and the pride of life according to 1 John 2:16. Don't be surprised to see pride and worldly lust gaining ground in your life if you are given to worldly fashion. If you are obsessed with the latest fashion and style, rather than running the heavenly race you were called into, you will find yourself running a race that God did not call you to.

The unfortunate thing about this is that those who are given to worldly fashion share a common destiny with what they are given to. Are you following fashion or Christ? In *Judges 8:24 the bible record the following account "And Gideon said unto them, I would desire a request of you, that ye would give me every man the earrings of his prey (For they had golden earrings, because they were Ishmaelites)*

WATCH WHAT YOU WEAR

At creation, God never considered the issue of dressing as something of a primary importance because there was no need for it. After the disobedience of Adam and Eve in the Garden of Eden, trouble came. In order to enable the couple to cover their nakedness, God clothed them.

Going by this gesture, it was clear that the primary purpose of clothing is to cover human nakedness. God the original designer only made coats of skin for Adam and Eve. However over the ages, human designers have perfected so many designs for different purposes, which is clearly beyond covering our nakedness to something else. Today, a walk across the streets in our cities and towns reveal so much about the way we dress. We can use the following acronym to describe dress.

D-Discipline

R-Respect

E-Elegant

S-Smart

S-Spirit Filled

Discipline: God is concerned about what you wear Exodus 28:47 and that is why He gave a specification of what it should look like and what language the dress should speak and impression it should give. If our dress does not meet God's specification, then we are careless. The lord said ladies should stop wearing spitted skirts. If we still insist on it, we are careless and not disciplined.

Respect: The dress of a child of God must carry glory, you cannot wear what you like- but what will bring glory to God I Cor. 10:31. A research has proved that 33% of how people are judged within 10 seconds is based on physical appearance and body language.

Elegant: Your garment must be beautiful. We are ambassador of Christ. We are His Excellency Prov. 31:22. Smell nice, make your hair neat. Be conscious of your choice of colours; it doesn't take too much to look nice. Being elegant does not make one flamboyant or to become worldly.

Smart: Wear smart but not tight dresses. Don't wear transparent dresses.

Spirit Filled: Be mindful of who makes you dress; take nothing for granted. Don't spend your money on "Faded Glory"; your glory will continue to shine in Jesus name. Let your breast remain inside your dresses keep your hips covered inside your dress. Let your life and dressing challenge the people spiritually and not carnally. Remember that the new dress of today is tomorrow's rag.

PUT ON YOUR BEAUTIFUL GARMENTS

Beautiful garments are to be worn; they are not for decorating the wardrobe or suitcase. If God has given you beautiful garments, put them on. If you do not wear your beautiful garment, someone else will wear them for you or share them among themselves or it will become outdated.

NEW GARMENTS FOR A NEW LEVEL

Dress the way you want to be addressed. Sometimes, a person's outlook speaks volumes about that person's status and a change of status often reflects in a change in outlook (Esther 2:17; Luke 16:19-31).

Mad men have their fashion, but it changes when they change (Mark 5:2-5, 15) Prostitutes announce themselves by their attire (Proverb 7:10) the high priest is easily distinguished by his garments of glory and beauty. (Exodus 28:2, 40) Garments are eloquent CV's of their wearers. Garments says a lot about you, what is it that differentiates a military from civilians; nurse from patients in the hospital; prisoners from warders; manager and labourers; a waiter from a guest and a pilot from a passenger? It is their mode of dressing.

In our passage, Zion was about to move up to a new and higher level; a level above "the uncircumcised and unclean"; a new level to which those trespassers would no longer have access. That new level was to be marked by the new outlook that Zion was to do something practical about: putting on her neglected beautiful garments that may have been hanging sorrowfully, as it were, 'by the rivers of Babylon.'

CHAPTER 3: GET BACK YOUR IDENTITY

Why did Jesus first change the name of Peter? For Peter's destiny to change for better, also bad names cannot produce a good destiny. Likewise, enemies change people's names or their victims in order to perpetrate evil in their life. For instance, every slave that has been captured, they will change their name in order to make them captive for life.

In Genesis 32:24-31, the bible tells the story of how Jacob got a new identity. *"And Jacob was left alone; and there wrestled a man with him until the breaking of the day. And when he saw that he prevailed not against him, he touched the hollow of his thigh; and the hollow of Jacob's thigh was out of joint, as he wrestled with him. And he said, let me go, for the day breaketh. And he said, I will not let thee go, except thou bless me. And he said unto him, what is thy name? And he said, Jacob. And he said, Thy name shall be called no more Jacob, but Israel: for as a prince hast thou power with God and with men, and hast prevailed. And Jacob asked him, and said, tell me, I pray thee, thy name. And he said, wherefore is it that thou dost ask after my name? And he blessed him there. And Jacob called the name of the place Peniel: for I have seen God face to face and my life is preserved. And as he passed over Penuel the sun rose upon him, and he halted upon his thigh.*

Also in Genesis 17:4-22, Abram's name was changed to father of nations. Let us look at the account. *"As for me, behold, my covenant is with thee, and thou shalt be a father of many nations. Neither shall thy name any more be called Abram, but thy name shall be Abraham; for a father of many nations have I made thee. And I will make thee exceeding fruitful, and I will make nations of thee, and kings shall come out of thee. And I will establish my covenant between me and thee and thy seed after thee in their generations for an everlasting covenant, to be a God unto thee, and to thy seed after thee. And I will give unto thee, and to thy seed after thee, the land wherein thou art a stranger, all the land of Canaan, for an everlasting possession; and I will be their God. And God said unto Abraham, Thou shall keep my covenant therefore, thou, and thy seed after thee in their generations. This is my covenant, which ye shall keep, between me and you and thy seed after thee; every man child among you shall be circumcised.*

And ye shall circumcise the flesh of your foreskin; and it shall be a token of the covenant betwixt me and you. And he that is eight days old shall be circumcised among you, every man child in your generations, he that is born in the house, or bought with money of any stranger, which is not of thy seed. He that is born in thy house, and he that is bought with thy money, must be circumcised: and my covenant shall be in your flesh for an everlasting covenant And the uncircumcised man child whose flesh of his foreskin is not circumcised, that soul shall be cut off from his people; he hath broken my covenant. And God said unto Abraham, As for Sarai thy wife, thou shalt not call her name

Sarai, but Sarah shall her name be. And I will bless her, and give thee a son also of her: yea, I will bless her, and she shall be a mother of nations; kings of people shall be of her. Then Abraham fell upon his face, and laughed, and said in his heart, Shall a child be born unto him that is an hundred years old? And shall Sarah, that is ninety years old, bear? And Abraham said unto God, O that Ishmael might live before thee! And God said, Sarah thy wife shall bear thee a son indeed; and thou shall call his name Isaac and I will establish my covenant with him for an everlasting covenant, and with his seed after him. And as for Ishmael, I have heard thee: Behold, I have blessed him, and will make him fruitful, and will multiply him exceedingly; twelve princes shall he beget, and I will make him a great nation. But my covenant will I establish with Isaac, which Sarah shall bear unto thee at this set time in the next year. And he left off talking with him, and God went up from Abraham.

ENEMIES CAN CHANGE YOUR IDENTITIES

In Daniel 1:6-7, it was recorded that Daniel, a man with an excellent spirit name was later changed by the enemy to Belteshazer which means prince of BAL to truncate his destiny. The three Hebrew boys name; Shedrach, Meshach and Abednego was changed to Hananiah, Misharel and Azariah.

Jedidiah was the name David gave Solomon but until he changed his name back to Solomon he did not succeed 2 Samuel 12:24-25 and 1Chronicles 22:8-13.

Identity problems begin by accepting the lie of the enemy. You were created in God own image. The greatest and fastest crime in the world today is identity theft. It begun from the beginning:

In Genesis 27; Jacob stole the identity of Esau. Also in 1King 3:16-28 there was an exchange of a living child with the dead one. In Genesis

29:21-27, Laban exchange Rachel for Leah because she was the older of the sisters.

CHAPTER 4: THE YORUBA NAMING CEREMONY

The Yoruba are one of the largest ethnic groups in West Africa. Majority of the Yorubas are in Western Nigeria. There are also established Yoruba communities in Antigua and Barbuda, the Bahamas, Barbados, Benin, Brazil, Cuba, Dominica, Ghana, Grenada, Guyana, Haiti, Jamaica, Puerto Rico, Sierra Leon, Trinidad and Tobago, Togo and the USA.

The naming of a child is a very important part of the Yoruba culture. A child's name is often derived from the circumstances of birth. Names are typically selected by family elders, though members of the community can also pay to name a child. The naming ceremony, wherein the community welcomes the child and accepts joint responsibility for raising him or her, occurs between 7 and 9 days after the birth of the child.

The key participants in the ceremony are usually the child, the father, the mother, family elders, grandmothers, grandfather, and the parents' siblings, particularly the mother's younger sister and an elder sibling or brother of the father. Honoured guests and community members also attend.

The elder then presides over the rest of the ceremony, which involves presenting the child with seven core symbolic items. Traditionally, the items are rubbed against the child's lips, but the modern approach to this practice involves the mother tasting the items on behalf of the child. The core items; water, salt, honey and or sugar, palm oil, kola nut, bitter kola, pepper, and dried fish. All these are symbolic.

The child's names are then given starting with the grandparents and parents, and afterward by the wider community. All the names of the child are called out, and repeated by the community. There are more prayers. The ceremony concludes with food, dancing and celebration to honour this new life.

The Bible clearly stated that you shall be called a new name. Let consider what the bible says in Isaiah 62:1-5. "*For Zion's sake will I not hold my peace, and for Jerusalem's sake I will not rest, until the righteousness thereof go forth as brightness, and the salvation thereof as a lamp that burn. And the Gentiles shall see thy righteousness, and all kings thy glory: and thou shall be called by a new name, which the mouth of the LORD shall name. Thou shall also be a crown of glory in the hand of the LORD, and a royal diadem in the hand of thy God. Thou shall no more be termed Forsaken; neither shall thy land any more be termed Desolate: but thou shall be called Hephzibah, and thy land Beulah: for the LORD delight in thee, and thy land shall be married. For as a young man marries a virgin, so shall thy sons marry thee: and as the bridegroom rejoices over the bride, so shall thy God rejoice over you.*

Also in Luke 1:30-35, the bible makes us to realize the importance of name. "*And the angel said unto her, Fear not, Mary: for thou hast found favour with God. And, behold, thou shall conceive in thy womb, and bring forth a son, and shall call his name JESUS. He shall be great, and shall be called the Son of the Highest: and the Lord God shall give unto him the throne of his father David. And he shall reign over the house of Jacob for ever; and of his kingdom there shall be no end. Then said Mary unto the angel, how shall this be, seeing I know not a man? And the angel answered and said unto her, The Holy Ghost shall come upon thee, and the power of the Highest shall overshadow thee: therefore also that holy thing which shall be born of thee shall be called the Son of God*".

CHAPTER 5: YOU SHALL BE CALLED BY A NEW NAME

God attaches great significance to names. It is unfortunate that many people don't pay attention to the importance of the names they bear or the names they give to their children. Africans, like the Jews, consider the meaning of a name before they give it to their children or to someone else.

The Name that the Almighty God chose to give to His only begotten Son is very significant. It is a wonder-working Name. In Matthew 1:21, we are told the reason the miracle child Mary would give birth to should bear the Name Jesus; "And she shall bring forth a Son, and thou shall call his name JESUS: for he shall save his people from their sins".

The promise of God for you is that He will change your name. How can this be possible? If you are barren and suddenly you are pregnant, you definitely witness sudden change. If you suddenly buy a car or a house; your name has changed automatically. If you are single and now married; your name has change. Remember God says I will not rest until I make you praise in the land. What is that problem in your life that people have identified you with that people use to describe you.

Brethren don't agree with Satan by answering that bad name but seek for the name that God calls you. Read Gen. 17:15, 32:26-28, Isa. 62:4a. There are many of us that have agreed with Satan that they can't prosper. Today, I want you to disagree with the devil and believe in God's word. John 11:39-40 and Luke 1:37 say for with God nothing shall be impossible.

God did not call you poor; some people will say that is my destiny. Problem is not your destiny or cross; God says I will not hold my peace for your sake. If today, it looks as if your heavens are closed; just read what Bible have for you in II Chr. 7:13-14. You can just do that now by kneeling on your feet and ask God to change your name and to forgive your sins. He will surely revive your destiny, land, business and family.

The promise of God for you this month is that He will change your name. What is a name? What is the meaning of your name? Who gave you that name? What is the power in a name? Why do you need new name?

CHAPTER 6: THE POWER OF NAME AND THEIR MEANING

Names are as powerful as the brake is to car. If you are in another city and somebody calls your name, you will automatically stop. Let us consider this account in Exodus 2:10. *"And the child grew, and she brought him unto Pharaoh's daughter, and he became her son. And she called his name Moses: and she said, because I drew him out of the water".*

Moses means, 'drawn out of water'. All his life goes round water; he turned water to blood, he parted the sea, he brought water from a rock, he turned bitter water to sweet and he never made it to the promise land because of water.

The bible record in Proverbs 18:10 that "t*he name of the LORD is a strong tower: the righteous runneth into it, and is safe.* What we can infer from this is that names given to our children have the power to make or mar their destiny. When you call on the name of Jesus, you are safe from the claws of the wicked ones. All impossibilities become possible; demons flee at the mention of this name. In short, the name is powerful and can move mountain.

Jeremiah 33:9 also attests to this. *"And it shall be to me a name of joy, a praise and an honour before all the nations of the earth, which shall hear all the good that I do unto them: and they shall fear and tremble for all the goodness and for all the prosperity that I procure unto it".*

Why do you need new name?

You need a new name for the promise of God to come to pass in your life. Until Abraham, Sarah, Jacob, Peter and Saul changed their names, the promise of God almost eluded them. In Genesis 33:1, Esau sent 400 hired killers against Jacob but thank God that overnight Jacob name was changed to Israel so God disappointed them. Abram remained barren till his name was changed. Peter was unstable in life and business that is why Jesus had to change his name fast.

Situations, problems, sickness and ungodly religion of your parents are what gave you that name. For instance, because you have not built a house of your own; people call you tenant. Is that your name?

HOW CAN YOU GET A NEW NAME?

The promise of God for you is that He will change your name. How can this come to pass? If you are barren and suddenly you get pregnant, that is the beginning of your change of name. If you suddenly buy a car or a house; your name will change. Once you get married as a young lady, your name will change. Remember, God says I will not rest until I make you praise in the land. What is that problem in your life that people have been calling you; blind man, jobless; remember it is not your name; it is the name that Satan, the enemy has given you. What name does God call you? *Genesis*

17:5 says; for a father of many nations have I made you.

Brethren don't agree with Satan by accepting that bad name but stick to the name that God calls you. Genesis 17:15, 32:26-28, Isaiah 62:4a. There are many of us that have agreed with Satan that they can't prosper. Today, I want you to disagree with devil and believe in God's word. John 11:39-40 and Luke 1:37 tell us that with God nothing shall be impossible.

Problem is not your destiny or cross. God says I will not hold my peace for your sake. If today, it looks like your heavens are closed just read what the bible has for you in *2 Chronicles 7:13-14; it says "If God shut the heaven and no blessings, you can re-open the heavens by turning away from your wicked ways in order to prosper".* You can just do that by going on your knees and ask God to change your name and to forgive all your sins. He will surely revive your destiny, land, business and family.

Investigate the meaning of your name and the real interpretation, who or what do they name you after. Perhaps you were named: Iyabo, Ekaete, Esugbayi, Ogunbiyi, Osuntuyi, Ifalana. Etc. brethren I am not condemning you but this can limit you. Some years ago I have dog and I named her Success but others in our environment call their dogs: spark, jack, bin-laden, killer etc. When I woke up I see success but what do my neighbors see?

CONDITIONS FOR NEW NAME

Let us critically consider what the bible says in Genesis 32:27-28; *"and he said unto him, what is thy name? And he said, Jacob. And he said, Thy name shall be called no more Jacob, but Israel: for as a prince hast thou power with God and with men, and hast prevailed".*

Jacob stood alone with God after he separated himself from all pleasure, worldly pursuit, family and all he has got in life, and told the angel the truth. Accept Jesus into your life today.

Also, if you confess your sins and have that absolute believe in God, He will give you a new name and new identity. Romans 10:8-11

CHOOSING A BIBLICAL NAME FOR YOUR BABY

Bringing a new person into the world is a life-changing experience. There are so many things to learn and so many decisions to make– among them, which name do you give to your child. It is not an easy task considering he or she will bear this name for the rest of his or her life.

Don't choose the name of your least favourite person or a name that brings up bad memories for you. Don’t just say my husband and I both love Rachel, but then we know this woman. Trust me, our future daughters are better off not being named Rachel. The same applies for the names of ex-girlfriends and boyfriends.

Do you have a religious belief or family traditions about naming your child after a family member? Some religions do, and in fact, some religions require that the person you are naming your child after is deceased. Some people prefer to give their children names that sound familiar.

SOME CHRISTIAN NAMES, SOURCE AND MEANING

Aaron (Hebrew) - Ex. 4:14 - a teacher, lofty, enlightener, mountain of strength.

Abel (Hebrew) - Gen. 4:2 – vanity, breath, vapour.

Abiathar (Hebrew) - 1 Sam. 22:20 - excellent father, father of the remnant.

Abigail (Hebrew) - 1 Sam. 25:3 - the father's joy.

Abihail (Hebrew) - 1 Chron. 2:29 - the father is strength.

Abihu (Hebrew) - Ex. 6:22 - he is my father.

Abijah (Hebrew) - 1 Chron. 7:8 - the Lord is my father.

Abishai (Hebrew) - 1 Sam. 26:6 - the present of my father.

Abner (Hebrew) - 1 Sam. 14:50 - father of light.

Abraham (Hebrew) - Gen.17:5 - father of a great multitude.

Abram (Hebrew) - Gen. 11:27 - high father; exalted father.

Absolom (Hebrew) - 1 Kings 15:2 - father of peace.

Adah (Hebrew) - Gen. 4:19 - an assembly.

Adam (Hebrew) - Gen. 3:17 – earthy, red.

Adina (Hebrew) - 1 Chron. 11:42 – adorned, voluptuous, dainty, slender.

Adonijah (Hebrew) - 2 Sam. 3:4 - the Lord is my master.

Adriel (Hebrew) - 1 Sam. 18:19 - the flock of God.

Alexander (Greek) - Mark 15:21 - one who assists men, defender of men.

Amaziah (Hebrew) - 2 Kings 12:21 - the strength of the Lord.

Amos (Hebrew) - Amos 1:1 – loading, weighty.

Ananias (Greek, from Hebrew) - Acts 5:1 - the cloud of the Lord.

Andrew (Greek) - Matt. 4:18 - a strong man.

Angela (Greek) - Gen. 16:7 - Angelic.

Anna (Greek, from Hebrew) - Luke 2:36 – gracious, one who gives.

Apollos (Greek) - Acts 18:24 - one who destroys, destroyer.

Aquila (Latin) - Acts 18:2 - an eagle.

Ariel (Hebrew) - Ezra 8:16 – altar, light or lion of God.

Artemis (Greek) - Acts 19:24 - whole, sound.

Asa (Hebrew) - 1 Kings 15:9 – physician, cure.

Asaph (Hebrew) - 1 Chron. 6:39 - who gathers together.

Asher (Hebrew) - Gen. 30:13 - happiness.

Atarah (Hebrew) - 1 Chron. 2:26 - a crown.

Azariah (Hebrew) - 1 Kings 4:2 - he that hears the Lord.

Barak (Hebrew) - Judges 4:6 - thunder, or in vain.

Barnabas (Greek, Aramaic) - Acts 4:36 - son of the prophet, or of consolation.

Bartholomew (Aramaic) - Matt. 10:3 - a son that suspends the waters.

Baruch (Hebrew) - Neh. 3:20 - who is blessed.

Bathsheba (Hebrew) - 2 Sam. 11:3 - the seventh daughter, the daughter of satiety.

Benaiah (Hebrew) - 2 Sam. 8:18 - son of the Lord.

Benjamin (Hebrew) - Gen. 35:18 - son of the right hand.

Bernice (Greek) - Acts 25:13 - one that brings victory.

Bethany (Hebrew) - Matt. 21:17 - the house of song, the house of affliction.

Bethel (Hebrew) - Gen. 12:8 - the house of God.

Beulah (Hebrew) - Isaiah 62:4 - married.

Bildad (Hebrew) - Job 2:11 - old friendship.

Bilhah (Hebrew) - Gen. 29:29 - who is old or confused.

Boaz (Hebrew) - Ruth 2:1 - in strength.

Cain (Hebrew) - Gen. 4:1 - possession, or possessed.

Caleb (Hebrew) - Num. 13:6 - a dog, a crow, a basket.

Candace (Ethiopian) - Acts 8:27 - who possesses contrition.

Carmel (Hebrew) - Joshua 12:22 - circumcised lamb, harvest; full of ears of corn.

Charity (Latin) - 1 Cor. 13:1-13 - dear.

Chloe (Greek) - 1 Cor. 1:11 - green herb.

Christian (Greek) - Acts 11:26 - follower of Christ.

Claudia (Latin/ Latin) - Acts 11:28, 2 Tim. 4:21 - lame.

Cornelius (Latin) - Acts 10:1 - of a horn.

Damaris (Greek, Latin) - Acts 17:34 - a little woman.

Dan (Hebrew) - Gen. 14:14 – judgment, he that judges.

Daniel (Hebrew) - 1 Chron. 3:1 - judgment of God, God my judge.

David (Hebrew) - 1 Sam. 16:13 - well-beloved, dear.

Deborah (Hebrew) - Judges 4:4 - word; thing, a bee.

Delilah (Hebrew) - Judges 16:4 - poor; small, head of hair.

Demetrius (Greek) - Acts 19:24 - belonging to corn, or to Ceres.

Diana (Latin) - Acts 19:27 - luminous, perfect.

Dinah (Hebrew) - Gen. 30:21 – judgment, who judges.

Dorcas (Greek) - Acts 9:36 - a female roe-deer.

Drusilla (Latin) - Acts 24:24 - watered by the dew.

Ebenezer (Hebrew) - 1 Sam. 4:1 - stone or rock of help.

Eden (Hebrew) - Gen. 2:8 – pleasure, delight.

Elah (Hebrew) - 1 Sam. 17:2 - an oak, a curse; perjury.

Eleazar (Hebrew) - Exodus 6:25 - the Lord will help, court of God.

Eli (Hebrew) - 1 Sam. 1:3 - the offering or lifting up.

Elihu (Hebrew) - 1 Sam. 1:1 - he is my God himself.

Elijah (Hebrew) - 1 Kings 17:1 - God the Lord, the strong Lord.

Eliphaz (Hebrew) - Gen. 36:4 - the endeavour of God.

Elisha (Hebrew /Latin) - 1 Kings 19:16; Luke 1:5 - salvation of God.

Elizabeth (Hebrew) - Luke 1:5 - the oath, or fullness, of God.

Elkanah (Hebrew) - Exodus 6:24 - God the zealous, the zeal of God.

Elnathan (Hebrew) - 2 Kings 24:8 - God hath given, the gift of God.

Emmanuel (Latin, Hebrew) - Isaiah 7:14 - God with us.

Enoch (Hebrew) - Gen. 4:17 – dedicated, disciplined.

Ephraim (Hebrew) - Gen. 41:52 – fruitful, increasing.

Esau (Hebrew) - Gen. 25:25 - he that acts or finishes.

Esther (Hebrew) - Esther 2:7 – secret, hidden.

Ethan (Hebrew) - 1 Kings 4:31 – strong, the gift of the island.

Eunice (Greek) - 2 Tim. 1:5 - good victory.

Eva (Hebrew) - Gen. 3:20 – living, enlivening.

Ezekiel (Hebrew) - Ezekiel 1:3 - the strength of God.

Ezra (Hebrew) - Ezra 7:1 - help; court.

Faith (Latin) - 1 Cor. 13:13 – loyalty, belief.

Gabriel (Hebrew) - Dan. 9:21 - God is my strength.

Gera (Hebrew) - Gen. 46:21 - pilgrimage, combat, dispute.

Gershon (Hebrew) - Gen. 46:11 - his banishment, the change of pilgrimage.

Gideon (Hebrew) - Judges 6:11 - he that bruises or breaks, a destroyer.

Grace (Latin) - Prov. 3:34 – favor, blessing.

Habakkuk (Hebrew) - Hab. 1:1 - he that embraces, a wrestler.

Hadassah (Hebrew) - Esther 2:7 - a myrtle, joy.

Hagar (Hebrew) - Gen. 16:1 - a stranger, one that fears.

Haggai (Hebrew) - Ezra 5:1 - feast; solemnity.

Hannah (Hebrew) - 1 Sam. 1:2 - gracious; merciful; he that gives.

Honey (Old English) - Psalm 19:10 - nectar.

Hope (Old English) - Psalm 25:21 - expectation; belief.

Hosea (Hebrew) - Hosea 1:1 - saviour; safety.

Huldah (Hebrew) - 2 Kings 22:14 - the world.

Hur (Hebrew) - Exodus 17:10 - liberty; whiteness; hole.

Hushai (Hebrew) - 2 Sam. 15:37 - their haste; their sensuality; their silence.

Immanuel (Hebrew) - Isaiah 7:14 - God with us.

Ira (Hebrew) - 2 Sam. 20:26 - watchman; making bare; pouring out.

Isaac (Hebrew) - Gen. 17:19 - laughter.

Isaiah (Hebrew) - 2 Kings 19:2 - the salvation of the Lord.

Ishmael (Hebrew) - Gen. 16:11 - God that hears.

Issachar (Hebrew) - Gen. 30:18 - reward; recompense.

Ithamar (Hebrew) - Exodus 6:23 - island of the palm-tree.

Jabez (Hebrew) - 1 Chron. 2:55 - sorrow; trouble.

Jacob (Hebrew) - Gen. 25:26 - cheater; that supplants, undermines; the heel.

Jael (Hebrew) - Judges 4:17 - one that ascends.

Jair (Hebrew) - Num. 32:41 - my light; who diffuses light.

Jairus (Hebrew) - Mark5:22 - my light; who diffuses light.

James (Hebrew) - Matt. 4:21 - same as Jacob.

Japheth (Hebrew) - Gen. 5:32 - enlarged; fair; persuading.

Jason (Hebrew) - Acts 17:5 - he that cures.

Jasper (Greek) - Exodus 28:20 - treasure holder.

Javan (Hebrew) - Gen. 10:2 - deceiver; one who makes sad.

Jemimah (Hebrew) - Job 42:14 - handsome as the day.

Jeremiah (Hebrew) - 2 Chron. 36:12 - exaltation of the Lord.

Jeremy (Hebrew) - 2 Chron. 36:12 - exaltation of the Lord.

Jesse (Hebrew) - 1 Sam. 16:1 - gift; oblation; one who is.

Jethro (Hebrew) - Exodus 3:1 - his excellence; his posterity.

Jewel (Old French) - Prov. 20:15 - delight.

Joab (Hebrew) - 1 Sam. 26:6 - paternity; voluntary.

Joanna (Hebrew) - Luke 8:3 - grace or gift of the Lord.

Joash (Hebrew) - Judges 6:11 - who despairs or burns.

Job (Hebrew) - Job 1:1 - he that weeps or cries.

Jochebed (Hebrew) - Exodus 6:20 - glorious; honourable.

Joel (Hebrew) - 1 Sam. 8:2 - he that wills or commands.

John (Hebrew) - Matt. 3:1 - the grace or mercy of the Lord.

Jonah (Hebrew) - Jonah 1:1 - a dove; he that oppresses; destroyer.

Jonathan (Hebrew) - Judges 18:30 - given of God.

Jordan (Hebrew) - Gen. 13:10 - the river of judgment.

Joseph (Hebrew) - Gen. 30:24 - increase; addition.

Joses (Hebrew) - Matt. 27:56 - raised; who pardons.

Joshua (Hebrew) - Exodus 17:9 - a saviour; a deliverer; the Lord is Salvation.

Josiah (Hebrew) - 1 Kings 13:2 - the Lord burns; the fire of the Lord.

Josias (Hebrew) - 1 Kings 13:2 - the Lord burns; the fire of the Lord.

Jotham (Hebrew) - Judges 9:5 - the perfection of the Lord.

Joy (Old French, Latin) - Heb. 1:9 - happiness.

Judas (Latin) - Matt. 10:4 - the praise of the Lord; confession.

Jude (Latin) - Jude 1:1 - the praise of the Lord; confession.

Judith (Hebrew) - Gen. 26:34 - the praise of the Lord; confession.

Julia (Latin) - Romans 16:15 - downy; soft and tender hair.

Justus (Latin) - Acts 1:23 - just or upright.

Keturah (Hebrew) - Gen. 25:1 - incense; fragrance.

Laban (Hebrew) - Gen. 24:29 - white; shining; gentle; brittle.

Lazarus (Hebrew) - Luke 16:20 - assistance of God.

Leah (Hebrew) - Gen. 29:16 - weary; tired.

Lemuel (Hebrew) - Prov. 31:1 - God with them, or him.

Levi (Hebrew) - Gen. 29:34 - associated with him.

Lillian or Lily (Latin) - Songs 2:1 - elegant flower; innocence; purity; beauty.

Lois (Greek) - 2 Tim. 1:5 - better.

Lot (Hebrew) - Gen. 11:27 - wrapped up; hidden; covered; myrrh; rosin.

Lucas (Greek) - Col. 4:14 - luminous; white.

Luke (Greek) - Col. 4:14 - luminous; white.

Lydia (Greek) - Acts 16:14 - a standing pool.

Magdalene (Greek) - Matt. 27:56 - a person from Magdala.

Malachi (Hebrew) - Mal. 1:1 - my messenger; my angel.

Manasseh (Hebrew) - Gen. 41:51 - forgetfulness; he that is forgotten.

Mara (Hebrew) - Exodus 15:23 - bitter; bitterness.

Marah (Hebrew) - Exodus 15:23 - bitter; bitterness.

Marcus (Latin) - Acts 12:12 - polite; shining.

Mark (Latin) - Acts 12:12 - polite; shining.

Martha (Aramaic) - Luke 10:38 - who becomes bitter; provoking.

Mary (Hebrew) - Matt. 1:16 - rebellion; sea of bitterness.

Matthew (Hebrew) - Matt. 9:9 - given; a reward.

Matthias (Hebrew) - Acts 1:23 - the gift of the Lord.

Melchizedek (Hebrew, German) - Gen. 14:18 - king of justice; king of righteousness.

Mercy (English) - Gen. 43:14 - compassion, forbearance.

Merry (Old English) - Job 21:12 - joyful, light-hearted.

Micah (Hebrew) - Judges 17:1 - poor; humble.

Micaiah (Hebrew) - 1 Kings 22:8 - who is like to God?

Michael (Hebrew) - Num. 13:13 - poor; humble.

Michal (Hebrew) - 1 Sam. 18:20 - who is perfect? Who resembles God?

Miriam (Hebrew) – Exodus 15:20 - rebellion.

Mishael (Hebrew) - Exodus 6:22 - who is asked for or lent.

Mordecai (Hebrew) - Esther 2:5 - contrition; bitter; bruising.

Moses (Hebrew) - Exodus 2:10 - taken out; drawn forth.

Myra (Greek) - Acts 27:5 - I flow; pour out; weep.

Nadab (Hebrew) - - Exodus 6:23 - free and voluntary gift; prince.

Nahum (Hebrew) - Nahum 1:1 - comforter; penitent.

Naomi (Hebrew) - Ruth 1:2 - beautiful; agreeable.

Naphtali (Hebrew) - Gen. 30:8 - that struggles or fights.

Nathan (Hebrew) - 2 Sam. 5:14 - given; giving; rewarded.

Nathanael (Hebrew) - John 1:45 - the gift of God.

Nehemiah (Hebrew) - Neh. 1:1 - consolation; repentance of the Lord.

Nekoda (Hebrew) - Ezra 2:48 - painted; inconstant.

Neriah (Hebrew) - Jer. 32:12 - light; lamp of the Lord.

Nicodemus (Greek) - John 3:1 - victory of the people.

Noah (Hebrew) - Gen. 5:29 - repose; consolation.

Obadiah (Hebrew) - 1 Kings 18:3 - servant of the Lord.

Olive (Latin) - Gen. 8:11 - fruitfulness; beauty; dignity.

Omar (Arabic, Hebrew) - Gen. 36:11 - he that speaks; bitter.

Onesimus (Latin) - Col. 4:9 - profitable; useful.

Oprah (Hebrew) - Judges 6:11 - dust; lead; a fawn.

Orpah (Hebrew) - Ruth 1:4 - the neck or skull.

Othniel (Hebrew) - Joshua 15:17 - lion of God; the hour of God

Paul (Latin) - Acts 13:9 - small; little.

Paula (Latin) - Acts 13:9 - small; little.

Peter (Greek) - Matt. 4:18 - a rock or stone.

Philemon (Greek) - Phil. 1:2 - loving; who kisses.

Philip (Greek) - Matt. 10:3 - warlike; a lover of horses.

Phineas (Hebrew) - Exodus 6:25 - bold aspect; face of trust or protection.

Phinehas (Hebrew) - Exodus 6:25 - bold aspect; face of trust or protection.

Phoebe (Greek) - Rom. 16:1 - shining; pure.

Prisca (Latin) - Acts 18:2 - ancient.

Priscilla (Latin) - Acts 18:2 - ancient.

Rachel (Hebrew) - Gen. 29:6 - sheep.

Rebecca (Hebrew) - Gen. 22:23 - fat; fattened; a quarrel appeased.

Reuben (Hebrew) - Gen. 29:32 - who sees the son; the vision of the son.

Rhoda (Greek, Latin) - Acts 12:13 - a rose.

Rose (Latin) - Song of Sol. 2:1 - a rose.

Ruby (English) - Exodus 28:17 - the red gemstone.

Rufus (Latin) - Mark 15:21 - red.

Ruth (Hebrew) - Ruth 1:4 - drunk; satisfied.

Samson (Hebrew) - Judges 13:24 - his sun; his service; there the second time.

Samuel (Hebrew) - 1 Sam. 1:20 - heard of God; asked of God.

Sapphira (English) - Acts 5:1 - that relates or tells.

Sarah (Hebrew) - Gen. 17:15 - lady; princess; princess of the multitude.

Sarai (Hebrew) - Gen. 17:15 - my lady; my princess.

Saul (Hebrew) - 1 Sam. 9:2 - demanded; lent; ditch; death.

Selah (Hebrew) - Psalm 3:2 - the end; a pause.

Serah (Hebrew) - Gen. 46:17 - lady of scent; song; the morning star.

Seth (Hebrew) - Gen. 4:25 - put; who puts; fixed.

Shadrach (Babylonian) - Dan. 1:7 - tender, nipple.

Sharon (Hebrew) - 1 Chron. 5:16 - his plain; his song.

Shem (Hebrew) - Gen. 5:32 - name; renown.

Sherah (Hebrew) - 1 Chron. 7:24 - flesh; relationship.

Shiloh (Hebrew) - Joshua 18:8 - peace; abundance; his gift.

Shiphrah (Hebrew) - Exodus 1:15 - handsome; trumpet; that does good.

Silas (Latin) - Acts 15:22 - three, or the third.

Simeon (Hebrew) - Gen. 29:33 - that hears or obeys; that is heard.

Simon (Hebrew) - Matt. 4:18 - that hears; that obeys.

Solomon (Hebrew) - 2 Sam. 5:14 - peaceable; perfect; one who encompasses.

Stephen (Greek) - Acts 6:5 - crown; crowned.

Susanna (Hebrew) - Luke 8:3 - lily; rose; joy.

Susannah (Hebrew) - Luke - lily; rose; joy.

Thaddaeus (Aramaic) - Matt. 10:3 - that praises or confesses.

Theophilus (Greek) - Luke 1:3 - friend of God.

Thomas (Aramaic) - Matt. 10:3 - a twin.

Timothy (Greek) - Acts 16:1 - honour of God; valued of God.

Titus (Latin) - 2 Cor. 2:13 - pleasing.

Tobiah (Hebrew) - Ezra 2:60 - the Lord is good.

Tobias (Hebrew) - Ezra 2:60 - the Lord is good.

Uriah (Hebrew) - 2 Sam. 11:3 - the Lord is my light or fire.

Uzziah (Hebrew) - 2 Kings 15:13 - the strength, or kid, of the Lord.

Victor (Latin) - 2 Timothy 2:5 - victory; victor.

Zacchaeus (Hebrew) - Luke 19:2 - pure; clean; just.

Zachariah (Hebrew) - 2 Kings 14:29 - memory of the Lord

Zebadiah (Hebrew) -1 Chron. 8:15- portion of the Lord; the Lord is my portion.

Zebedee (Greek) - Matt. 4:21 - abundant; portion.

Zebulun (Hebrew) - Gen. 30:20 - dwelling; habitation.

Zechariah (Hebrew) - 2 Kings 14:29 - memory of the Lord.

Zedekiah (Hebrew) - 1 Kings 22:11 - the Lord is my justice; the justice of the Lord.

Zephaniah (Hebrew) - 2 Kings 25:18 - the Lord is my secret.

Zerubbabel (Hebrew) - 1 Chron. 3:19 - a stranger at Babylon; dispersion of confusion.

The Nigerian local names and their meanings:

	Danladi	Hausa	Born on Sunday	M/F
	Mekudi	Hausa	Money owner	M/F
	Nathaniel	Hausa	Perfume Seller	M
	Useni	Hausa	Junior twins child	M
	Yakere	Hausa	It's finished	M/F
	Tijani	Hausa	Given	M
	Ubah	Ibo	Wealth	M
	Okechukwu	Ibo	My share from God	M
	Ijeoma	Ibo	Go well	F
	Igbokwe	Ibo	If Igbo agree	M

	Okona	Ibo	The father's favourite	F
	Ndidi	Ibo	Patience	F
	Ngozi	Ibo	Blessing	F
	Nwobodo	Ibo	A citizen	M
	Ahamefule	Ibo	Let my name not lost	M
	Nnamdi	Ibo	My father is alive	M
	Abiola	Yoruba	We've given birth	M
	Oluwasegun	Yoruba	God has conquered	M
	Kumuyi	Yoruba	Death don't take	M
	Akin	Yoruba	Hero	M
	Bolanle	Yoruba	Born into wealth	F
	Femi	Yoruba	Love	M/F
	Funmi	Yoruba	Gift	F
	Tokunbo	Yoruba	Born across the sea	M/F
	Adesuwa	Edo	Amidst wealth	F
	Akhigbe	Edo	Not to be killed	M
	Bilulu	Edo	What have I done	M
	Ese	Edo	A gift	M/F
	Efosa	Edo	Wealth	M/F

	Esosa	Edo	God's gift	M/F
	Ogeneovo	Urhobo	God is one	M/F
	Ochuko	Urhobo	Helper	M/F
	Ubeku	Urhobo	Strong	M
	Okpoko	Urhobo	Elder/leader	M
	Uwen	Efik	Life	M
	Okon	Efik	Night	M
	Uduak Obong	Efik	God's Purpose	M
	Abasido	Efik	God is with me	M
	Emem	Efik	Peace	F
	Ekaete	Efik	First daughter	F
	Imabong	Efik	God's Love	F
	Achibong	Efik	Blessing	F

CHAPTER 7: CONTENT OR CONTAINER

Your name is that container that can rebrand you. Do you know that a container can add or disvalue the content? In the history of human race, there has never been anyone just like you. The odds of another human being having your unique combination of characteristics and qualities are more than 50 billion to one. This means that you have the potential to do something special or extraordinary with your life; something that no one else can do. However, the question is: are you going to do it? It's true that some people are born with rare, unique gifts, but most of us are introduced to life with average talents and abilities.

Those individuals the society labelled "great" reached high levels of performance by developing their talents to a very high degree in the field of their choice. In other words, your potential lies dormant if you don't make use of it. It must be identified and developed if you hope to get more out of life. Make your own choices before life makes them for you.

If you are going to have a new future, you need a new beginning. If you are going to realize a new destiny, you will need a point of origin. Of all the questions asked by those who dare to succeed, one stands above the rest: "I want to succeed, but how?" The answer is simple: by utilizing your greatest gift. No life ever grows great until it is dedicated, disciplined, and focused!

It is not all that glitters that is gold. We have pure gold and gold-plaited iron, and it is very hard to know the difference. Whenever you get an offer, you need to pray very well and seek God's face, so that you will not accept an offer that will later enslave you. This offer might come in different form and shape. It might be a job offer, with fat salary, fantastic dressing allowance, nice car and housing allowance. No matter how attractive it may look like, just ensure, that it is not an invitation into slavery. Also, before you accept that proposal from that man, make sure that it is not an invitation into slavery. Don't just look at how handsome he is, how buoyant he is, what type of car he uses and the type of mansion he lives in; marriage is more than just looking at the container; be mindful of the content also.

Some make friends with the wealthy and highly placed, and such friendship later landed them in secret cults; what a bondage? Genesis 44: 9-10 says 'hurry and go up to my father, and say to him, thus says your son Joseph: "God has made me lord of all Egypt; come down to me and do not tarry. You shall dwell in the land of Goshen, and you shall be near to me, you and your children, your children's children, your flocks and your herd, and all that you have".

Furthermore, Exodus 1: 9 & 11 says, "and he said to his people, look the people of the children of Israel are more and mightier than we; therefore they set taskmasters over them to afflict them with their burdens. And they built for pharaoh supply cities, Pithom and Raamses."

The offer for the children of Israel to come down to Egypt looked good and it looks like an invitation from lack to abundance, but it was also an invitation from freedom to slavery. May the Holy Spirit, give us the wisdom to discern and know the right offer to take. "What is your real worth or value"?

Most of the time, people try to underestimate our real worth or value. They place a very low premium upon us. They try to undervalue us. If you think that a pure gold is just a mere gold-plaited iron, you might have sold it cheap before you realise the real value or real worth of the gold. In Genesis 37:28, Joseph was sold to the Ishmaelites for just 20 shekels of silver. "Then Midianite traders passed by; so the brothers pulled Joseph up and lifted him out of the pit, and sold him to the Ishmaelites for twenty shekels of silver". A future prime minister was sold for just 20 shekels of silver. Someone, who will eventually control the wealth of a nation and even the whole world- who would eventually save them from famine, was sold for a ridiculous amount.

Most of the time, people place little or no value upon us. They refuse to value our talents. They refuse to value the grace of God upon our lives. They refuse to value our dreams and they refuse to value our personality. But I have good news for you; It is not the value that the world place upon you that matters, but the value that God places upon you. Joseph dream of becoming great, his future ambition and his personality only worth just 20 shekels of silver to his brothers.

Jesus personality as the saviour of the world only worth just 30 pieces of silver to Judas Iscariot and the Jews. The king of kings and the lord of lords was betrayed to those who will later kill him, for just 30 pieces of silver. But Jesus said, "what shall it profit a man if he gains the whole world and loses his soul" (Mark 8:36). It means that you are worth more than all the riches and wealth of the whole world put together. Jesus knew his worth. That was why he refused to bow down for Satan when he promised him all the riches of the world. Do you also know your worth? Think about it.

In Christian service, God only rewards FULFILLMENT and not ACHIEVEMENTS. Achievements are means to an end while fulfilment is the ultimate. What's the specific purpose of God for your life and how far have you gone in fulfilling it? Don't be carried away with the various achievements God gives- they are to motivate, encourage and inspire you to remain faithful and committed to the purpose. Until the dry bones receive the breath of life and rise to become exceedingly great army, you have not yet fulfilled the purpose of God. May God help you to remain faithful and focused on the purpose till you fulfil it eventually.

What guarantees your great fulfilment and strong finishing in the Christian race is not only your attempt of the purpose of God, but your determination to remain faithful, diligent and persevere till the end. The reward only comes at the end and for those who through patience endure to complete the race. May the gracious Lord give you divine strength to show the same diligence till the end no matter the cost. Amen

ABOUT THE AUTHOR

Joel Odunayo Daramola whom God raised from grass to grace, has pioneered many parishes in The Redeemed Christian Church of God.

Currently: As Assistance Provincial Pastor Admin in Lagos province 37.

A graduate of The Redeemed Christian Bible College (RCBC), School of Disciple (SOD) and Institute of Leadership.

He holds a B.A. (Ed) in Guidance and Counseling from the prestigious University of Lagos (UNILAG).

He is a teacher who is registered with the teacher's registration council of Nigeria (TRCN)

A trained R & A Engineer (thermodynamics) with over 30 years' experience.

He is the CEO, Ayo-Technical Services (ATS). & Vision Link For You and I.

He is the host of Power Service (a weekly breakthrough and deliverance service) for over two decades.

A prolific writer, author of many books; a respected Evangelist, a gifted prophet with vast insight into the word of God.

Publisher of the Monthly Journal: "VISION LINK" for more than 20 years.

He has the vision to challenge young people to actualize their potentials in life.

His mandate is to spread the word of God, raise disciples, and build them to maturity for the perfection of saints through God's empowerment.

A prolific speaker, dexterous writer and a leading voice in Ministry and Leadership circles,

He is sought as a Conference speaker across the globe. His ministry is in high demand by both denominational and non-denominational ministries alike as his ability to engage people with God's word and effective prayer

He is passionate about raising people who are thoroughly steeped in Kingdom values and very relevant in the Secular world.

He believes that Christians should be able to influence society with kingdom principles.

His fine blend of excellence and spirituality has made him stand out from the pack.

He believes God has a plan for everybody and that God can take the most unlikely and use him powerfully.

A Youth leader, an administrator, entrepreneur and motivational speaker with a global vision.

A motivational speaker for over two decades. He has organized seminars and conferences to inspire the Youths in schools and Church for Nation building, Vision discovery and career advancement. His fine blend of excellence and spirituality has made him stand out from the pack, he believes that God has a plan for everybody and that God can make use of anyone powerfully.

He has published many books; Sounds of the abundance of rain; At the darkest hour; Are you passing through? Destined for greatness but tied down among others.

He is happily married to Pastor (Mrs.) C.O. Daramola and their union is blessed with four Children: Power, Queen, Excellence and Great.

Emails: pastordara@yahoo.com & visionlinkdara1@gmail.com

Phone & WhatsApp +2348033275896.

Facebook: Joel Odunayo Daramola

Websites: www.visionlink4u.com

www.ingramcontent.com/pod-product-compliance
Lightning Source LLC
LaVergne TN
LVHW050335160826
845677LV00014B/3623